Peace, Love, And A Turtle Dove

Hope Gallup

Presentation by *BookLeaf Publishing*

Web: www.bookleafpub.com

E-mail: info@bookleafpub.com

ISBN: 9789357745147

First edition 2023

I dedicate this book to The Greatest Gift I have Ever Had, My Turtle Dove,

Sophia Sonja. Without you, to help me, who would I be? Just a Half, YES exactly!

Love,

Your Momma, HMG

ACKNOWLEDGEMENT

I would like to take this time to Acknowledge BookLeaf Publishing for launching this contest for all of us poets or writers that competed, and all the other contestants that tried, great job! It wasn't easy! Also, I would like to say thanks to all of my English teachers throughout the years. I actually won a spelling bee at Westwood Elementary School for my class. It wasn't easy! But being a good speller and reading a ton as a child makes writing kind of easy. So, thanks to my English Teachers. Thanks to my mother who always took my sister and myself to the library every week. I really did love my mysteries. I read a ton of Arthur Conan Doyle, and Agatha Christie in my formative years. They were my favorites. I was a bit of a mystery dork. Still am. As I got older, I graduated into the long-winded and weird Stephen King, and James Patterson, but bumped back to MC Beaton's Mysteries, and a few other corny ones also. Then I moved on to more Art related and creativity-related projects. Branching out to woodburning, mosaics, home improvement projects, etc. I am a top-notch home painter and take extreme pride in anything I try. Refining and seeking perfection, borderline OCD does run in the family! Thanks Mom But my work ethic stemmed from Dad also. I would like to acknowledge my best mentor, Greg King. He helped me become a great leader and I admire him. He used to leave me the best notes! So, to anyone that may have been an inspiration for any of the poems, thank you. Without you in my life, this would not have been possible. Good or bad, without you, who would I be? This I see.

PREFACE

I think that this book is a way for me to summarize my life in a way that just made sense to me. Some of the poems were about what I went through during my divorce, like Exiled in the D. Others were about me as a person. I learned a lot about myself as I began this contest and had to quantify so many of them to fit the challenge, and make them flow into the contest. The titles say it all, Like Dangerous When Wet, or My Angel. Lover, One More Time Around, see what I mean? I'm sure you can find something you may relate to. So, I filled in the blanks as I went. I realized how "Dr. Seuss'y my writing really was. By golly, I just figured I should embrace it, and that is when I ended up writing the Ode to the Doctor himself. I have always wanted to write a book and this was the opportunity I have been looking for. I am about seizing opportunities lately when I see them. Why not, you just never know. I was diagnosed with a benign brain tumor about 10 years ago. Tomorrow isn't always guaranteed. Stay busy, live life! I hope you enjoy something within the poems or can relate to something. Thanks for reading. Peace, Love, and I hope you see a Turtle Dove.

THE PHOENIX DOVE

Hey, I'm like that bird.
You know the One
They tried to burn down.
Yeah, that one.
Yet I rise every day Yes!
And I will Try!
Yes, Every day I Rise!
I Fly! I Survive!
For Peace, Love, And A Turtle Dove.

SOMETIMES I SLEEP

Yes, now I sleep all by myself.
No longer do I feel your flesh, so lovely.
Some nights I really don't sleep.
Yearning for your hot flesh next to me, on top of
me, all over me.
All on me.
But now I just sleep.
Sometimes barely.
All by myself.
And it gets easier.
My heart is free.
I'm free to be me.
My mind.
My body.
All by myself.
Sometimes I sleep.
Finally.

Sometimes I Sleep

THE FEATHER IN AWE

I am the Beautiful Feather.
Stuck in his craw.
I once was the feather in a great white snow owl.
Now I am perched on the head of the Great
Chief,
And I am in AWE.
I am just a little feather.
For one means nothing, but TOGETHER,
WE STAND STRONG..
IN REMEMBRANCE OF ALL.

BROKEN WIRE

Here it comes...
I see it movin' up up, and through the wire!
It is electric, like the absolute hottest fire!
It tastes so delicious, I think!
So close now, almost here, I need a drink! I'm on
the Goddamn brink!
I'm charged up, so excited I'm jumpin'!
My heart is a thumpin', ears are burnin', cheeks
red, lips are crimson...
The spark is movin' faster now, Oh thank you
Mr. Electrician!
Here's the spark! And then, just my luck!
Nothin'!
Broken Wire!

DRIVE ME LORD

Dear Lord, Grant me The Will
To NOT stomp on the Gas That Holds My
Tongue,
And Tell Them What I Truly Think!
That Will Get Me Nowhere Fast!
My Tongue is Sore from The Constant Biting,
And Has the Most Exquisite Taste.
Yes, Lord, Grant me the Patience
To NOT Stomp on the Gas And run them All
Down,
For Their Seriously Unfair Ways!
I Have Endured This Unequaled Opportunities
and Wages
And Expect Not a Lot to Change, it's
unfortunate, whatever they may say.
I still have to ask for the same wage, they don't
just give it. I'm worth it for sure.
I work hard and have earned it.
Come on! I have more experience! More miles,
come on!
My humbleness keeps me from showing and
glowing.
Good thing I also have poetry! And I finally love
myself a little, too.

Yes, thank you Lord, you get me. You have given me the grace and DRIVE me Lord to endure and not run them all over! Thankfully!

Love,
Hopey

MY ODE TO THE ADOPTED

To all the adopted souls who may be having a
bad day...
Their minds tend to go to...
Where do I spring from? Is my family near me?
Or quite far away?
See, my daddy was adopted, and I am sure that
he felt that way.
He once mentioned his was named Charles, they
changed it to Ronald that day.
He was Viking, Nordic, mild-mannered in every
way. He was a fighter, had that twinkle in his
eye. That charm you can't deny.
I like to believe Mr. Keith could be my Grampa,
yes, he's the Man!
You can pick someone too. A relative to admire.
Maybe a woman.
It could be a sister, a Grammy, to help get you
through, when you're feeling blue....It's all up to
you.

MY ANGEL

GOD gave me YOU because he knew my life
wouldn't be easy.
You always ARE and are THERE to be my
SOUL LANTERN.
You light UP and show me the way just by
LISTENING.
You ALWAYS HAVE.
THANK YOU for listening. And in RETURN,
you showed me HOW TO LISTEN.
Oh my FRIEND, you have GUIDED and
COMFORTED ME so wonderfully and
MOLDED ME into the human I am today.
Together, we have endured our sorrows, and
humiliations, and grew through
our adversities. The wolves and lions tried to
bite our souls
with their cruelties but ho! We are the warriors!
They would not conquer us! Now my most
precious Turtle Dove and I fight to death. Fight,
fight, fight!
My angel, My Sister To Death, Fight, Fight,
Fight! Bound by Friendship
We stand Cleaved by Blood. I will fight for our
Voices in Life
and Love you Now and In Death!

My Angel on Earth,
Thank you!

LOVER ONE MORE TIME AROUND

Couldn't See The Good
So He did Go, Yes, Flee
He Ran From "Us" From "We".
Yes he ran from the edge
And straight into the bright new moon.
That whispered to him
"Yes, she is your one true lover, give her one
more time around!"
So he ran Straight into
Her Sexy Eyes
That Spoke to Him
"Oh, Lover, Thank you, Yes!"
That's How "We Should Be!"

DANGEROUS WHEN WET

Throw water on me,
And you will see,
That I catch like a missile,
Being shot into space,
There is no stopping me!
You must not know who
You are dealing with,
To want to spark this explosive material
Without Warning;
I am Extremely Dangerous When Wet,
You must like that a little;
I am assuming you want to play with me?
How touching! I hope you packed a big lunch.
It's going to be a long day fella.
I come with a placard label.
I am Extremely Dangerous When Wet.
But You Will Enjoy It.
EXCLUSIVELY, Maybe.
HAZARDOUSLY a little, you will see.....Love,
HMG

EXILED IN THE "D".

Oh, surely is this going to be the new me?
I refuse to see myself as an Exilee? Is that a
word?
I hope not, Oh, surely!
I made tough choices.
I went for broke.
I did something for ME. And Sophie.
I did what was right, you see?
For a change, it was about time, frankly.
Now I am stronger, and so is she.
even though I am mostly alone.
It feels better, natural, comfortable.
I am Enlightened.
I will always have my Turtle Dove.
Her song revives me, so peacefully.
I got fed up, beat up, messed up,
Then finally I moved up.
Now I am Free!
Thankfully!

MY ODE TO DR. SEUSS

Now here we go with Sophie Joe, Or Yertle
Turtle, is what her Momma
always gurgles. On a Wacky Wednesday, I will
try to remember, Yes of
course, it was the 1st of Octember. Soph was
thinking, Oh the Thinks You
Can Think! when all of a sudden she sees a Cat
in a Hat eating Green Eggs and Ham. Gross she
thought. When she turns to see Mrs. Brown
yelling at Andy the Fox in Sox that Mr. Brown
Can Moo, Can You? Andy, who is part of The
Lorax family, said "If I Ran the Zoo, I would
make sure that Everyone had a Wocket in Their
Pocket when they left the zoo, and a cotton
candy too! Come on Mr. Brown, Hop On Pop, I
will give you a ride, Oh, the Places We'll Go!
Let's Go Dog Go! I am so Happy and Thankful
Things are gonna happen for you and me and
Sophie Joe! Here We Go!

THE GHOST, MY ONLY FRIEND

This old ghost, just a man, that had the nerve to
leave me!
Kept me believin' then poof! Gone!
It kept happening! He was always fooling me!
Yes, he was Ghosting Me!
Then that old Ghost became my bestie, I cried so
much to him.
We became Lovers, I believe, that Old Ghost
and Me.
He came round so consistently.
Time went by, I grew stronger, the ghost grew
bored as well.
I said Listen, Ghost I love me Most, I made
peace, so hit the street! I don't Miss that Ghost,
but I'm ok with me, so it's OK, yes, Goodbye,
Ghost.

OF THE DAY

At the beginning of the day I choose You.
Then I go about to do the things I do.
The people, the places, the wide open spaces.
The ridiculous in abundance, the over
abundance.
Then I close it, and motor back home to "It".
We Both Know This.
We Have Went Through our Trials
We Both Had our Troubles.
Now We Know About It
And What To Do, So At The
End of The Day,
I choose to Lose All My Clothes to You.
My Skin Becomes One With You.
It is the Best Part of the Day Babe.
Yes, the Best Part.....
OF THE DAY.

WHAT JEFFREY MEANT
TO ME

He was there in the beginning,
And that was the world to me.
He was the kindest when he wanted to be.
And the hottest, oh yes, was he!
But, the tides, they turned,
and the sadness, I did see.
Oh, Jeffrey, what you meant to me.
Now I am filled with sadness,
and a pain in my chest, where you stabbed me...
cause you wounded me...over and over, so
brutally.
But I let you again and again. Thinking:
Maybe you would see How Good I am.
Oh, Jeffrey, why didn't you see?
I was loyal to you, yet always you counted all of
my imperfections and impossibilities!
You broke my heart and I let you get the best of
me.
I was weak, but at last, now I am free!
Oh, Jeffrey, what you meant to me!
Gone Forever,
Goodbye,
Hope Marie

MY COMPEER

Where is My Compeer? I ask as I awake from my deep sleep.
I am looked at quizzically, almost accusingly. I fall back asleep.
There is my companion! He is there always accompanying me, when I need him to be. No one knows how much I love my HEARTY! He is my Heart's Treasure! Worth more than Gold to Me! My Compatriot! My Confederate! He is So Special To Me! I Make Him So So Happy! If I didn't, That would Kill Me! My Compeer, My Lover, XOXO, Faithfully.

REMEMBER ME

I am With You Now,
And Will Always Be.
Standing Beside You,
Bound by Our Family Tree.
So, When You Hear the Wind,
Whispering Through the Trees,
It's Me Saying "I Miss You."
Just Smile and Remember Me.
Go Find Our Special Place
By The River, Under the Oak Tree
Lock Up the Love and Leave.
Then Walk Away and Smile,
And Just Remember Me.

Remember Me

MOTHER

She is my truth and loves me no matter. Oh, mother, for you have made my life.
You are my namesake, and for God's sake, you have dealt with my good and my bad, and when I was so sad. You met all the boyfriends and saw all my real friends and fake friends and never said when friendships had to end! Oh, mother I adore you and will never ignore you. I will care for you and always be there for you. So, just so you know, thank you for being my mother.
There is certainly no other. You're 1000X more precious than gold. I hope you are proud, and we have many, many more days together, and both get really old!

THE REASON

REALLY, THERE IS ONLY ONE.
THE MOST CRUCIAL ONE, YOU SEE.
THE ONE THAT I BORNE.
THE ONE THAT HAS MY FULL DRAW.
THE ONE THAT HAS MY FULL PULL.
THE LIGHT THAT WILL NEVER FADE.
FOR IT IS SO BRIGHT TO ME.
THE LIGHT OF MY LIFE.
MY POWER, MY TRUE, TRUE SPIRIT I
FEEL
WHEN I AM WITH HER, AND SHE HUGS
ME.
THAT IS ALL I REALLY NEED. IF I COULD
AT
THAT MOMENT, I WOULD HAVE LIVED
AND DIED
THE MOST PERFECT WAY, FOR SHE MADE
IT, AND
GAVE ME THAT GIFT. THANK YOU, LORD,
FOR
GIVING ME HER, MY SOPHIA SONJA, THE
MOST
PERFECT BEING, AND "THE REASON" I
TRY SO
 HARD EVERY DAY.

I hope you also find some peace, love, and a
turtle dove by Hope Marie Gallup.

www.ingramcontent.com/pod-product-compliance
Lightning Source LLC
LaVergne TN
LVHW010831200726
843508LV00012B/2553